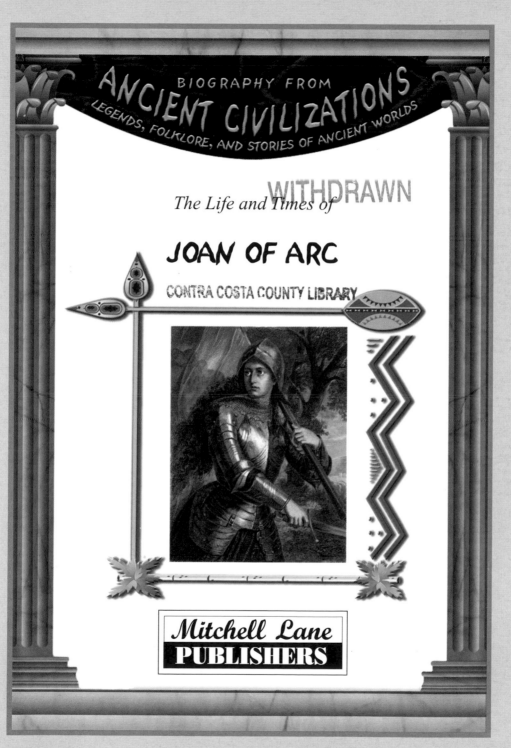

BIOGRAPHY FROM

ANCIENT CIVILIZATIONS

LEGENDS, FOLKLORE, AND STORIES OF ANCIENT WORLDS

The Life and Times of

JOAN OF ARC

Mitchell Lane
PUBLISHERS

P.O. Box 196
Hockessin, Delaware 19707

BIOGRAPHY FROM
ANCIENT CIVILIZATIONS
LEGENDS, FOLKLORE, AND STORIES OF ANCIENT WORLDS

Titles
in the Series

The Life and Times of:

BIOGRAPHY FROM
ANCIENT CIVILIZATIONS
LEGENDS, FOLKLORE, AND STORIES OF ANCIENT WORLDS

The Life and Times of

JOAN OF ARC

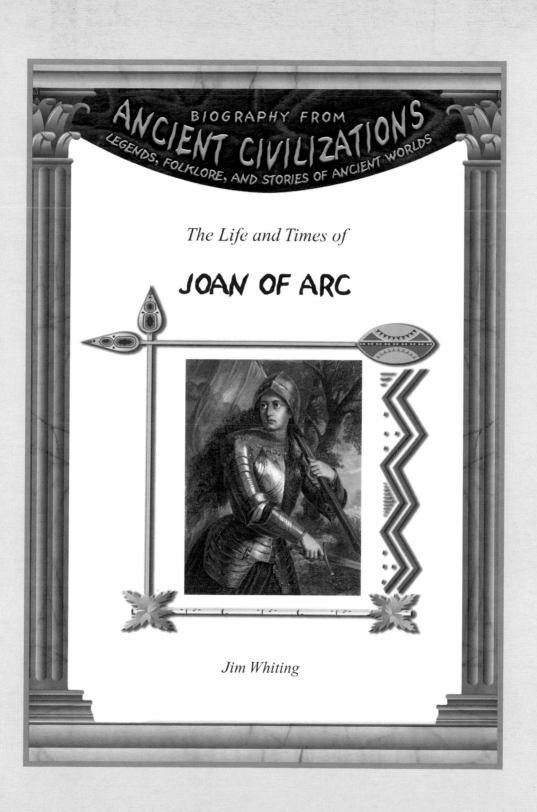

Jim Whiting

Mitchell Lane
PUBLISHERS

Printing   1   2   3   4   5   6   7   8

Library of Congress Cataloging-in-Publication Data

Whiting, Jim, 1943-
     The life and times of Joan of Arc / by Jim Whiting.
       p. cm. — (Biography from ancient civilizations)
     Includes bibliographical references and index.
     ISBN 1-58415-345-8 (library bound)
  1. Joan, of Arc, Saint 1412-1431—Juvenile literature. 2. Christian women saints—France—Biography—Juvenile literature. 3. Hundred Years' War, 1339-1453—Juvenile literature. 4. France—History—Charles VII, 1422-1461—Juvenile literature. I. Title. II. Series.
DC103.5.W44 2005
944'.026'092—dc22
                                    2004030260

ABOUT THE AUTHOR: Jim Whiting has been a journalist, writer, editor, and photographer for more than 20 years. In addition to a lengthy stint as publisher of *Northwest Runner* magazine, Mr. Whiting has contributed articles to the *Seattle Times*, *Conde Nast Traveler*, *Newsday*, and *Saturday Evening Post*. He has written and edited more than 160 Mitchell Lane titles. He lives in Washington state with his wife and two teenage sons.

PHOTO CREDITS: Cover, pp. 1, 3, 6 Getty Images; p. 9 Andrea Pickens; p. 10 Corbis; p. 14 Andrea Pickens; p. 22 Getty Images; pp. 25, 27, 28 Corbis; p. 32 Getty Images; p. 38 Library of Congress

PUBLISHER'S NOTE: This story is based on the author's extensive research, which he believes to be accurate. Documentation of such research is contained on pages 46-47.

The internet sites referenced herein were active as of the publication date. Due to the fleeting nature of some web sites, we cannot guarantee they will all be active when you are reading this book.

BIOGRAPHY FROM
ANCIENT CIVILIZATIONS
LEGENDS, FOLKLORE, AND STORIES OF ANCIENT WORLDS

The Life and Times of

JOAN OF ARC

*For Your Information

This image of Joan of Arc shows the armor that she wore in battle. The way that the artist composed this picture shows the importance of the banner she carried with her. Even though she also had a sword, she disliked killing. She preferred to lead her troops by inspiring them. Her banner often served as a rallying point for the men.

CHAPTER
ONE

A TANGLED WEB

On the morning of May 30, 1431, a nineteen-year-old girl was taken from a dark prison cell in Rouen, France. She had been held there for more than six months, often with heavy chains binding her. She had been imprisoned primarily because she claimed that she heard voices from God. Another reason was that she had worn men's clothing. She had been found guilty of those charges.

Now it was time for her punishment. Dozens of heavily armed soldiers escorted her to the central marketplace. Hundreds of townspeople watched the procession. Hundreds more packed the square.

When she arrived, she had to endure a barrage of insults from France's most important clergyman. In front of all those people, he called her a "snake," a "liar," "rotten," an "instrument of the devil." When he finished demeaning her, he allowed her a few minutes to pray. Then she was tied to a stake, which was surrounded by huge piles of firewood.

An executioner bent over the wood with a torch and set it alight. The flames quickly reached the girl. According to most witnesses, she didn't scream in pain. Instead, she continued to pray.

Soon her agony was over. Joan of Arc was dead before the fire consumed her body.

Joan of Arc is one of the most famous women in history. She is the patron saint of France. The National Library in Paris holds more than 20,000 books about her. Millions of television viewers tuned into the 1999 miniseries that starred Leelee Sobieski in the title role. The TV series *Joan of Arcadia* features a heroine who—like Joan—is a teenager and hears divine voices. In short, as biographer Mary Gordon says, "[Joan of Arc] may be the one person born before 1800, with the exception of Jesus Christ, that the average Westerner can name."[1]

Yet if only one of three short-lived French kings had had a son, it is likely that no one would have ever heard of Joan of Arc.

Joan's story begins nearly a thousand years before her birth. An early French king named Clovis, who ruled from 481 through 511, wrote sixty-five separate laws that collectively became known as the Salic Laws. They encompass many topics, ranging from murder to the theft of pigs, the stealing of fences, and the voicing of insults (calling another man a "hare" or a "fox," for example, would involve a financial penalty). Yet another law dealt with the way that property could be passed on. According to one of its provisions, "of Salic [French] land no portion of the inheritance shall come to a woman: but the whole inheritance of the land shall come to the male sex."[2]

During the following centuries, the Salic Laws were nearly forgotten. The stage for their revival came in 1314 with the death of King Philip IV. Each of his three sons—Louis X, Philip V, and Charles IV—ruled for brief periods before following their father in death. None of those three sons left behind any male heirs. The death of Charles IV in 1328 ended about 350 years of rule by the Capetian dynasty. It also ended the clear line of succession.

With Charles's death, two men claimed the French throne. One was another Philip. Known as Philip of Valois (pronounced val-WAH), he was the cousin of Charles IV and the nephew of Philip IV.

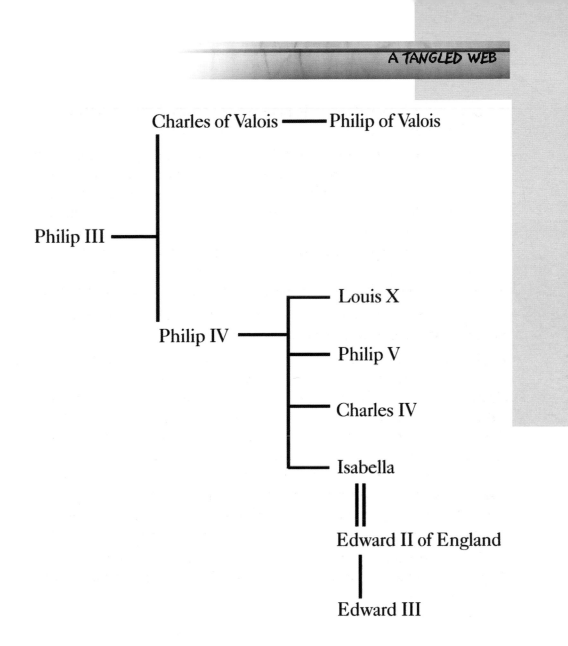

This family tree shows the rival claims to the French throne after the three sons of Philip IV died within a few years of each other. The English King Edward III was closer to Philip. But his claim came through his mother. In a male-oriented era, that was a serious handicap. The crown went to Philip of Valois, who was descended from Philip's younger brother Charles.

The French King Philip IV, also known as "Philip the Fair" because he was a good-looking man, was born in 1268. He was married in 1284 to a girl who was eleven at that time. Philip became king the following year. For much of his reign, he was in conflict with the Pope in Rome. He died in 1314 and was succeeded by his eldest son, who became Louis X.

The other was Edward III, the king of England. His father, Edward II, married Isabella, the daughter of Philip IV. In dynastic terms, that marriage made Edward III more closely related to Philip IV than Philip of Valois was. Under most circumstances that would have given Edward a clearer right to the throne.

However, his claim came through a woman, which seriously weakened it. French noblemen cited the long-disused Salic Law, even though it referred only to private property. Under their interpretation, the crown of France—the "inheritance" to which the Salic Law referred—had to go to a male. As a result, Philip of Valois became the king and ruled as Philip VI. Edward was unhappy, but there was little he could do about it.

His feelings changed in 1337 when Philip invaded the province of Gascony, located in southwest France. Gascony had been under English control for more than a century. At that point, Edward asserted his claim to the French throne. This began what became known as the Hundred Years' War (which actually lasted 116 years, finally ending in 1453). Very little happened for the first nine years. Then an English army invaded France and won an important victory at Crécy. Another important English victory took place a decade later at Poitiers. The French King John—who had succeeded Philip a few years earlier—was captured and taken to England, where he died in 1364. Now the English controlled vast tracts of French land.

But England couldn't take advantage of the situation. Under the leadership of Charles V—John's son—the French soon regained nearly all the territory they had lost. By 1375, the English controlled only Gascony and the port of Calais on the English Channel. By the time Charles VI succeeded his father in 1380, the French had begun a period of relative peace. It was shattered shortly after the turn of the century when a civil war broke out. Bands of armed men loyal to one side or the other roamed the French countryside, terrorizing the inhabitants.

The situation for the French got even worse when Henry V became the English king in 1413. A strong and vigorous ruler, he took advantage of the turmoil in France to lead a small army there two years later. He justified his invasion by saying that he was claiming his right to the French throne. He was the great-grandson of Edward III and therefore related to the long-dead Philip IV. It soon appeared that Henry had miscalculated. Two months after landing, with his men suffering from malnutrition and disease, he faced a French army that enjoyed a numerical superiority of about five to one. Against all odds, the English won an overwhelming victory at the Battle of Agincourt.

Over the next few years, Henry followed up his victory at Agincourt with a series of other triumphs that put most of northern France under his control. It helped that some French nobles were on his side. The most important was the Duke of Burgundy, whose father had been murdered several years earlier by forces siding with the French crown.

In 1420, Henry forced Charles VI to sign the Treaty of Troyes. Under its terms, Charles's son Charles—who was the dauphin (doe-FAN), or crown prince—was disinherited. Henry V became the heir to the French throne. To make his position stronger, Henry married King Charles's daughter Catherine. The following year the couple had a son. The war seemed on the verge of ending, but conditions changed radically in the summer of 1422 when Henry V died. He was only thirty-five. His infant son became Henry VI, the king of both England and France.

For the next six years, the tiny king's uncle, the Duke of Bedford, continued the string of English military successes with the aid of the Duke of Burgundy. Charles, the dauphin, continued to insist on his claim to the throne, but as the years went by the territory under his control steadily shrank. He became more and more discouraged. His treasury had less and less money. It seemed only a matter of time until he would be killed or captured. Then France would fall completely under the control of England.

A teenage girl in a small farming village was about to see that that didn't happen.

The Battle of Agincourt

Soldiers fighting at Agincourt

In mid-August 1415, Henry V landed near the French port of Harfleur with an army of less than 10,000 men. To his surprise, it took more than a month to capture the port. With autumn's cold and rainy weather approaching, Henry had to abandon his original plan of attacking Paris and go back home. To demonstrate his power to the French, he felt that he needed to march across part of the country rather than simply leave from Harfleur. The logical destination was the port of Calais, about 120 miles to the north.

The decision nearly proved to be disastrous. Henry and his men were forced to march more than 250 miles because superior French forces blocked the direct route. Finally they were cornered near the village of Agincourt. By then, according to estimates, Henry had only about 5,000 men, while his opponents had 25,000. His men, already weakened by disease and lack of food, were further exhausted by so much marching. On top of everything else, they spent the night before the battle trying to sleep on open ground in a driving rain. Not surprisingly, the outlook for the English on the morning of October 25, 1415, was grim.

Henry had an unexpected ally: Mother Nature. The battlefield lay between two sets of dense woods, making it impossible for the French to surround him. The French were funneled into a relatively narrow front, less than 1,000 yards wide. The initial charge pushed the English back a little, but the French were packed so tightly that many literally couldn't even raise their weapons. The English began pushing them back. At the same time, more French troops pressed forward, making the congestion even worse. Wearing heavy armor, many slipped and fell on the wet ground. The English archers threw down their bows and swarmed over them with knives, clubs, and axes. Thousands of French troops were slaughtered without being able to defend themselves. English losses were a few hundred.

Henry won a great victory. The name Agincourt became so powerful in the English imagination that Prime Minister Winston Churchill used it to hearten his fellow citizens during the darkest days of World War II.

This map of France shows the sites of the major events in Joan's life. These range from her birthplace in Domrémy to her trial and execution in Rouen. Her greatest triumph in battle took place at Orléans. She was especially proud of leading the dauphin Charles to Rheims where he was crowned as Charles VII.

CHAPTER

TWO

HEEDING THE VOICE OF GOD

Joan of Arc (or Jeanne d'Arc, as she is known in France) was probably born on January 6, 1412, to Jacques and Isabelle d'Arc in the village of Domrémy. Her father was one of the village's more prosperous farmers. He owned about fifty acres of land, and the family lived in a large stone house. Joan had three brothers—Jacquemin, Jean, and Pierre—and a sister, Catherine.

Normally we would know very little or nothing about someone— especially a female—with such a background during that era. Yet the circumstances of her life and death resulted in three very lengthy and searching examinations. As a result, we have extensive records—both in her own words and in the words of others—of the conditions under which she achieved her lasting fame.

The location of Joan's village played an important role in determining her fate. Situated on the eastern boundary of present-day France in the province of Lorraine, Domrémy lay on one side of the Meuse River—the side that favored Charles the dauphin. On the other side of the river the allegiance was to the Duke of Burgundy. The conflict appeared to affect everyone. Children in Domrémy frequently got into fistfights with youngsters from neighboring Maxey, which lay on the opposite bank of the Meuse.

For thirteen years, Joan lived a normal life. "I worked at common tasks about the house, going but seldom afield with our sheep and other cattle," she recalled several years later. "I learned to sew and spin. As to my schooling, I learned my faith, and was rightly and duly taught to do as a good child should."[1]

As a "good child," Joan did housework, took care of the sick, and helped out at harvest time. Occasionally there would be time for fun. She enjoyed going to what was known as the Fairies' Tree with her friends. The youngsters would make strings of flowers and hang them on the branches of the tree. Joan also spent considerable time in church. To some people, the amount of time she spent there and her level of devotion may have seemed a little excessive.

One of her childhood friends recalled, "She was very devout towards God and the Blessed Virgin, so much so that I myself, who was young then, and other young men, teased her."[2]

Another remembered, "She did not dance, so that we, the other girls and young men, even talked about it."[3]

Yet she was not a fanatic. The overall impression had by people who knew her as a child was of a strong and healthy girl, one who fit comfortably into the life of the village.

Then on one warm sunny day, everything changed.

"When I was thirteen, I had a voice from God to help me to govern myself," she said. "The first time, I was terrified. The voice came to me about noon: it was summer, and I was in my father's garden. I had not fasted the day before. I heard the voice on my right hand, towards the church. There was a great light all about."[4]

The first message was simple and straightforward: Be a good girl and God will help you. The voice continued to address Joan, sometimes coming to her as often as two or three times a week. Soon she was able to identify its source: It was the archangel Michael. As the months went by, she began feeling more comfortable in his presence.

Eventually her comfort level would be shattered. Michael told her that two other saints—Margaret and Catherine—would also speak to her. When they appeared as promised, they laid a heavy responsibility on her shoulders. God had a mission for her, they said. France was in deep trouble. She must leave her village, ride to the court of Charles the dauphin, then lead him to the city of Rheims, where he would be crowned king. Most of this perilous journey would take place through territory that was controlled by the Duke of Burgundy.

It must have been hard for Joan to believe her ears. "I answered the voice that I was a poor girl who knew nothing of riding and warfare."[5]

It didn't matter. The voices continued with their insistent message. They even began adding to it. They told her that her mission would begin in the town of Vaucouleurs. Its governor, Robert de Baudricourt, would provide her with an armed escort. As the voices continued to press her, Joan tried to maintain the appearance of a normal life. It was especially difficult because of her father. From a conversation with her mother, she knew that he would not permit her to leave the village.

"My mother had told me that my father often dreamed that I would run away with a band of soldiers," Joan said. "She told me that he had said to my brothers, 'If I believed that the thing I have dreamed about her would come to pass, I would want you to drown her; and if you would not, I would drown her myself.' On account of these dreams, my father and mother watched me closely and kept me in great subjection. And I was obedient in everything."[6]

Making her life even more difficult, her father tried to get her to marry a young man in the village when she was sixteen, a common age for marriage at that time. She told him that marriage was out of the question because she had taken a vow of chastity. What she didn't tell him was the reason she had made that vow. From the very beginning, the voice of St. Michael had insisted on it.

In our era, some people believe that claims of hearing "voices" show that the person is mentally unbalanced. Others have suggested that what Joan was hearing was actually her conscience. But Joan was acting in accord with common beliefs at the time.

"There was a well-established tradition of [particularly] holy women receiving divine revelations, which often brought them into public prominence,"[7] says writer Andrea Hopkins.

In any case, it doesn't really matter if the voices were "real" or "imaginary." Joan completely believed in them and listened to them for the rest of her life.

About that time, the danger to her country became very personal. Burgundian forces attacked Domrémy itself in the summer of 1428. Joan and the other villagers had to flee to the nearby town of Neufchâteau and take shelter behind its walls for a couple of weeks. The attack only added to the pressure she was under to make her escape.

Her father wasn't the only problem. At that time, it was unthinkable for a young woman to travel alone. She needed help to leave Domrémy. Then she had a stroke of good fortune. One of her cousins, Jeanne Laxart, who lived in a village close to Vaucouleurs, was expecting a baby early in 1429. Joan offered to help in the delivery. Her cousin's husband, Durand, came to get her. As soon as they left Domrémy, Joan explained the situation. Her enthusiasm quickly won him over. He guided her to Vaucouleurs, where she met with Baudricourt.

Baudricourt was not impressed with the girl who stood before him. He told Durand to take her back home. He suggested that her father give her a good spanking.

Though Joan returned to her cousin's house, she decided to go back to Vaucouleurs and try again. Again the answer was no. By this time the voices were becoming even more insistent. Joan decided on another strategy. Previously she had appeared wearing a dress. Now she put on some of Durand's clothing. Again she confronted

Baudricourt. She let him know that only a few hours earlier her voices had told her that the English had inflicted a serious defeat on the French, more than a hundred miles away. More than ever, the dauphin needed her help.

In an era when communication was measured by the speed of a horse, Baudricourt had no direct knowledge of such a battle. Nor did Joan. A few days later, messengers arrived with the dreadful news. The French had been defeated when and where Joan had said. Baudricourt was convinced that she had powers, either from God or from the devil. A brief examination assured him that her powers came from God. He gave her a sword and an armed guard to conduct her to the court of the dauphin in the city of Chinon. It lay more than 300 miles away. Several people expressed concern about the possibility of an unpleasant encounter with an enemy.

"I fear them not," she replied. "I have a sure road, for I have God with me, Who will prepare my way to the dauphin. To do this was I born."[8]

Her confidence was well founded. Eleven days later she and her party arrived safely in Chinon; they'd had no problems along the way. In Chinon, she was ushered into a large reception hall.

According to a popular legend, the dauphin wanted to test Joan. He exchanged clothes with one of his courtiers. Yet Joan, who had never seen him before, headed unerringly toward him. Joan later said that her voices directed her toward the dauphin, who was standing in the midst of a group of men. His appearance may have also helped her to locate him easily. Described as "the ugliest man in Christendom,"[9] Charles had a number of distinctive and well-known facial features.

Again she had to sell herself. There is a great deal of speculation as to what she said. Perhaps it had nothing to do with her words, but with her potential value as a symbol. The politically astute Charles might have recognized that his disheartened men needed a rallying point, something to ramp up their morale. Before he committed himself, however, he needed to satisfy himself that she was divinely inspired. He sent her to a group of clergymen, who subjected her to a series of rigorous questions. She was even examined physically to determine if she was a virgin.

"To the modern mind it may seem completely unimportant as to whether Jeanne were a virgin or no; not so in the fifteenth century," comments biographer W. S. Scott. "To people of that age it was a well-known and established fact that the Evil One [the devil] could have no dealings with a virgin; consequently an assurance on this point was urgently necessary."[10]

Joan passed all the tests. She was given the equipment she needed to carry out her mission: horses, a suit of white armor, and a banner, which the peace-loving girl said she loved forty times more than any sword. Despite her feelings about the relative value of a sword, she still had to have one. She said the one she wanted was buried behind the altar in a nearby church. No one else was aware of its existence. A man was sent to dig it up. It was there, just as she had predicted. There is, however, no evidence that she ever used it to kill anyone.

A few weeks before, she had been an ordinary peasant girl in a red dress, pleading with a dubious nobleman. Now clad in gleaming white armor, she was la Pucelle (lah pooh-SELL, or "the Maid").

One of the most glorious—and shortest—military careers was about to begin.

The Saints Who Spoke to Joan

FYI
For Your Info

It is a measure of the importance of Joan's mission that St. Michael was the angel who first spoke to her. In the Catholic Church, St. Michael is an archangel, which means that he is considered to be one of the most important angels. There are only seven of them, and Michael is one of just three—St. Raphael and St. Gabriel are the others—who are mentioned specifically by name in the Scriptures. St. Michael was the leader of the faithful angels when Lucifer, the devil, rose in rebellion against God. Because Lucifer and the rebel angels were defeated, St. Michael is considered to be a protector of the church.

Catherine of Alexandria, Egypt, con-fronted the Roman emperor Maximinus, probably sometime around 235 A.D., because he was mistreating Christians. He ordered her to be thrown into prison, where his wife and some soldiers visited her. When she con-verted them to the Christian faith, Maximinus had them executed. Then he ordered Catherine to be executed by being bound to a spiked wheel. When she touched the wheel, it disappeared as if by a miracle. Maximinus had her beheaded. Angels carried her to Mt. Sinai—the site where Moses received the Ten Commandments. A church and monastery were later dedicated there in her honor.

Catherine of
Alexandria, Egypt

Margaret of Antioch was born where Turkey is today, probably about 300 A.D. Her father was a pagan priest who disowned her when she adopted the Christian faith at an early age. As she grew older, she became very beautiful. A Roman official wanted to marry her. When she refused, he brought her to trial and insisted that she give up being a Christian. Again she refused to do his bidding. She was sentenced to be burned, but the flames had no effect on her. Then she was tied up and thrown into a huge kettle of boiling water. She still survived. Finally the official ordered her to be beheaded.

According to the *Catholic Encyclopedia,* St. Catherine and St. Marga-ret are regarded as among the fourteen most helpful saints.

This heroic picture of Joan of Arc emphasizes her leadership qualities and her sainthood. Like the picture on page 6, this one also focuses on her banner. But it contains one feature that isn't very accurate. In real life, of course, she didn't wear a dress into battle.

CHAPTER
THREE

FROM VICTOR TO VICTIM

Joan's objective was obvious. It was Orléans, one of the most important cities in France. Orléans was the gateway to the entire Loire Valley, one of the few areas still under French control. If the English captured it, Charles's position in Chinon would be gravely threatened.

The English had begun a siege of Orléans the previous October. While they didn't have enough men to completely encircle the city or to mount an attack, they controlled the one bridge across the Loire River that led into the city. They also maintained more than a dozen strongpoints.

Before departing for Orléans, Joan sent a challenge to her enemies: "Surrender to the Maid, who is sent here by God the King of Heaven, the keys of all the good towns you have captured and destroyed in France. . . . And you should know for sure that the King of Heaven will send more strength to the Maid than you are able to put together against her and her good soldiers in any attack."[1]

The English responded by telling her to go back home and tend her cattle.

The English weren't the only ones who downplayed her. It soon became apparent that there was a significant difference of opinion among her own people about her role. She envisioned herself leading men into battle. The French commanders—especially Jean, the cousin of Charles and leader of the Orléans garrison—envisioned her primary value as helping to lift the spirits of the men—sort of a mascot or a cheerleader, standing on the sidelines. Her value as an inspirational figure became obvious when Joan was able to slip into the city under cover of darkness in late April, 1429. She was greeted as a liberator by the citizens.

Jean was harder to convince. Even before they reached the city, he and Joan had gotten into an argument because she didn't approve of the route that he wanted to take with the badly needed supplies. She thought he was trying to avoid a fight with the English. He was also concerned that it would take a long time to get inside the city with the supplies. The plan was to put the supplies on boats and sail past the English, but the wind was blowing in the wrong direction. Jean was afraid that it could take several days for it to change. Joan excused herself and went down to the edge of the river to pray. Moments later, there was a strong gust and the wind began blowing in the right direction. Soon Joan and the others were in Orléans.

Despite this apparent evidence of Joan's unique abilities, Jean remained reluctant to allow an unproven teenage girl to fight among hardened soldiers. A week later, the French received word that hundreds of English troops were approaching to reinforce Fort Saint Loup, one of their strongpoints. Joan wanted to take a nap so that she would be rested for the upcoming fighting. She told Jean to awaken her when the battle was about to begin. He didn't. Suddenly she woke up. Her voices had told her to fight. She was furious at Jean for not waking her earlier. She quickly set off, accompanied by a few men. Her arrival was perfectly timed. The French were faring poorly and were about ready to retreat when they caught sight of her banner. Given new encouragement, they rushed the fort again, with Joan at their head. Within an hour they captured it. Her presence had turned the tide.

Napoléon Bonaparte was probably France's greatest military genius. Born in 1769, he rose to prominence in the mid-1790s. He became Emperor of France in 1804 and soon controlled most of mainland Europe. He lost the decisive Battle of Waterloo in 1815 and was exiled to a remote island in the Atlantic Ocean, where he died in 1821.

More than three centuries later, another famous French military leader, Napoléon Bonaparte, would say that moral factors in war—such as the willingness to fight and the level of confidence—were three times more important than physical factors—equipment, training, and so on. He might well have had Joan in mind.

Two days later, Joan played an important role in capturing another strongpoint, the Fort of the Augustines. Now that she had proven herself in battle, it was time to attack the key to the English position. This was Les Tourelles, a pair of fortified towers that controlled the bridge leading to the city.

The attack began on the morning of May 8, 1429. As the voices prophesied, Joan was wounded in the throat by a crossbow bolt soon after the fighting began. At first she kept going, but loss of blood soon forced her to stop. Rumors began to circulate among the French that she had been killed. They lost heart and began to retreat. Joan pulled out the bolt herself in what must have been agony and rushed back to the front line. Newly heartened, the French surged forward. The drawbridge and gate were set afire. Some English were killed in the assault. Others fell into the river and drowned. The survivors fled to nearby towns that their countrymen controlled. Orléans was again in French hands. Never again would the English be so close to conquering France.

Joan acquired still another name. La Pucelle became la Pucelle d'Orléans, or the Maid of Orléans.

Above all, as biographer Mary Gordon notes, "What the battle does indicate, indisputably, is her extraordinary physical courage and stamina. . . . Both for the French and for the English, she was a presence whose importance and power stemmed not from any traceable action or behavior but from an atmosphere that preceded and surrounded her. . . . The French needed someone like Joan, someone to break through their paralysis. She broke through and handed them victory. If she had not been victorious, the story would have ended there."[2]

Obviously, the story didn't end at Orléans. Joan's success convinced the pious French that God was with them. They fought with fresh enthusiasm. To solidify their position, the French had to drive the English out of several towns near Orléans where they had taken refuge. With Joan playing a major role, Jargeau fell on June 12. Then Meung-sur-Loire. Then Beaugency. Then Patay. All within the space of six days. The campaign became known as the "week of victories."

These victories were a double-edged sword. Joan was happy to free more French territory. She was unhappy by all the killing that was necessary to accomplish it. Once she saw a French soldier strike a vicious blow against an unarmed prisoner. She held the dying man and listened to his final confession.

Each battle, no matter how bloody, brought her closer to her goal: Rheims. This was the ancient city where French kings stretching

Clovis I is generally regarded as the first King of France. Born in 466, he became king of his tribe at the age of 15 and soon unified all the neighboring tribes. He became a Christian a few years later and was baptized at Rheims. Historians believe that he had the Salic Laws put on paper shortly before his death in 511.

back to the time of Clovis were traditionally crowned and anointed with holy oils. Joan wanted Charles to be honored in this way. She knew it was important for France to have a king, rather than a dauphin.

Somewhat surprisingly, Charles initially resisted the idea. The city lay about 150 miles northwest of Orléans, in territory sympathetic to the Duke of Burgundy. Joan was insistent, and Charles—still somewhat reluctantly—set off. This time there was little if any bloodshed as the French appeared before several major cities. It was a triumphant procession. Troyes fell. Then Châlons-sur-Marne. And finally Rheims. There was a bonus when Joan arrived there. Her father had preceded her. His earlier inclination to drown her must have disappeared when he realized what she had accomplished. It also helped that Charles gave him a gift of cash and also exempted the town of Domrémy from being taxed.

Born in 1403, Charles the dauphin was crowned King Charles VII at Rheims in 1429 with Joan's help. Her devotion to him gave him the nickname of Charles the Well-Served. A few years after Joan's death, Charles got rid of his advisers and replaced them with men who convinced him to become more active. It paid off because the Hundred Years War came to an end during his reign. He spent his final years fighting his son, who was crowned as Louis XI when Charles died in 1461.

As Charles received the crown, Joan kneeled proudly nearby, clutching her banner. With the dauphin now officially Charles VII, Joan wanted to continue the momentum that she had gained in the previous couple of months. Again Charles proved to be reluctant. He wanted to call a momentary halt to the fighting. He began negotiating with Burgundy for a truce.

Joan was very upset. She said she would oppose the truce. She was as good as her word. With a few hundred men, she launched an attack on Paris. This time she miscalculated badly. She thought the citizens of Paris would support her. They didn't. Again she was wounded. This time there was no almost instantaneous recovery. By the time she was ready to resume combat, her reputation had received a fatal wound. She had promised to take Paris. She hadn't. That began to cast doubts on her so-called divine mission.

Charles quickly broke off the attack and withdrew to Chinon. He disbanded most of the army. Joan was left with enough troops to continue campaigning in the Loire Valley, though she literally had to beg for money from several towns. In October, she took the town of St.-Pierre-Le-Moutier. It would be her final major victory, as she failed the following month to capture La Charite-sur-Loire. By this time Charles had concluded an even longer truce with Burgundy. Joan was forced to go back to Chinon to live with the idle courtiers. Depressed, she spent the rest of the winter quietly. It probably came as little compensation that Charles raised her family to the nobility, giving them a coat of arms that featured lilies and naming them Du Lis (pronounced doo LEE).

Campaigning began again the following spring. By then Charles realized that he had been duped. Burgundy had had no intention of working toward a peaceful settlement. He used the time to build up his army. Joan was sent to the town of Melun. It seemed as if her aura was back. As soon as she appeared, the town switched its allegiance from Burgundy to Charles. It was her last success. While she was still celebrating her triumph, St. Catherine and St. Margaret appeared to her. This time the news was depressing. You will be captured soon, they told her.

She learned of the desperate situation of the town of Compiègne, which lay a few miles northeast of Paris. It had refused to surrender to Burgundy as part of the truce agreement. Now it was besieged. Joan rode north, determined to help defend the town. To the great joy of the townspeople, she slipped inside its walls in mid-May. On the afternoon of May 23, she rode out to launch a surprise attack. But Compiègne was not destined to be another Orléans. Sizable English forces appeared from one direction and Burgundians from the other. Joan's men realized they would soon be trapped and fled back toward the town. The drawbridge was quickly lowered. Most of the men clattered across it to safety, then it was hurriedly raised. Joan, covering the retreat, was trapped outside. The governor of the town, Guillaume

The final scene in the 1957 movie "Saint Joan" shows actress Jean Seberg clutching a wooden cross that a kind guard gave her. The movie was the first film role for Seberg, who was born in 1938 in a small town in Iowa and was virtually the same age as Joan. The film's director, Otto Preminger, chose her from among thousands of applicants. She became a well-known actress and had numerous roles until her death in 1979. Among them was "Paint Your Wagon," in which Clint Eastwood was one of her co-stars.

CHAPTER
FOUR

A HORRIBLE DEATH, BY FIRE

When Joan's captors removed her from Beaurevoir, they took a roundabout route to Rouen. They stopped frequently along the way to humiliate Joan by displaying her as a prisoner to as many people as possible. She completed her miserable journey just after Christmas. Right away she received a terrible shock. She was thrown into an English civil prison. She was chained to a heavy log. Her guards were men.

That was just the beginning of a horrible few months. Joan quickly learned that she couldn't expect a fair trial. Bishop Pierre Cauchon, who conducted the proceedings, and the other judges were all loyal to the English. They drew up a long list of charges, most of which fell into two principal categories.

One category concerned her voices. She claimed that they contacted her personally and guided her. That contradicted the teachings of the church, which felt that it was solely responsible for explaining divine will to the people. There was no place for personal experience. There was also a political angle involved. Joan maintained that through the voices, she knew God supported the French in their struggle against the English. Cauchon would try to disprove this notion by "proving" that she was a witch, and therefore inspired by the devil, not by God. That would help the cause of the English and Burgundians.

The other main accusation was that she wore male clothes. Dressing like a man seems to have been especially alarming to the clergymen who tried her. It was directly against God's teachings and was offensive to God, they felt.

The trial began on February 21, 1431. Court reporters were careful to record every question that Joan was asked and her answers, leaving a very clear picture of what went on. Joan had no legal counsel. A girl who could neither read nor write, she was facing up to sixty of the most prominent clergymen in the region. Many if not most had been involved with the church before Joan had even been born.

Yet Joan refused to be intimidated. Many of her responses were brilliant. Over and over she heard the same questions about the nature of her voices and visions: what they looked like, what they wore, and the length of their hair. Even her wounds and seemingly miraculous escapes were used against her. She must have been a witch to survive such close calls, her accusers said.

"Her conduct during this ordeal, which is recorded minutely in the trial documents, was heroic," writes one of her biographers. "She spoke with [complete openness] to her accusers, just as she had spoken to dukes and counts at the height of her acclaim. Despite the appalling conditions in which she was kept she refused to be intimidated and answered her interrogators boldly, even contemptuously."[1]

Joan had little comfort as the weeks went by. Her voices kept telling her that she would somehow be saved, but the constant questioning began to wear away her resistance. She asked for the opportunity to say a mass. To be released from her chains. To be released from the constant threat of attack by her guards. All her requests were denied. Cauchon urged that she be tortured. In a rare demonstration of mercy, that suggestion was ignored. But the end was near.

Joan faced an impossible choice. If she pleaded guilty, she would be saying that she had lied about her voices, that her "divine mission" was simply a pack of lies. If she maintained her innocence, she would be condemned as a heretic—even worse, a heretic who refused to accept the truth.

On May 24 she was taken to a cemetery in Rouen. It was the first time that she had been outside in several months. It was also the first time since she had left Vaucouleurs more than a year before that she appeared in women's clothing. She stood next to a huge pile of wood and a stake. It was a vivid reminder of the cruel fate that awaited her. She had to listen to a long sermon from one of her accusers.

Finally she could take no more. She recanted, or took back, what she had said about her voices. At that moment, it must have seemed that anything was better than being burned alive. A document was thrust in front of her. It said that she agreed that she hadn't had the visions she had claimed to have. She signed it, agreeing that she would obey the will of the church and wear women's clothing from then on. She probably believed that after making this confession, she would be transferred to a church prison or maybe even set free.

The English and their Burgundian allies were furious. It appeared to them that Cauchon had allowed her to escape death. He told them not to worry. At his orders, Joan was taken back to the same prison. She quickly realized that she had been tricked. A lifetime of misery seemed to stretch in front of her. Within a few days, she put her male clothing back on.

Accompanied by several of the judges, Cauchon rushed to her cell. He demanded to know why she had broken her promise not to wear men's clothing again. Joan answered that she had not been transferred to a church prison. Then Cauchon asked if she had heard her voices again. Joan said yes. The voices had told her that by confessing, she had done something very wicked. The clerk who recorded the conversation made a note in the margin.

Responsio mortifera, he wrote. "Fatal answer."[2]

Joan had sealed her fate. Not only had she put on men's clothes again, she had also admitted that the voices had reappeared to her. That meant she had relapsed. Now there could be no "forgiveness."

On the morning of May 30, 1431, she was taken to the center of the Rouen marketplace. A dunce cap rested on her shaved head. With a stake surrounded by a huge pile of firewood looming in the background, Joan had to listen while Cauchon read out the final statement. She was given half an hour to pray. Some of the onlookers began to feel sorry for her. Others grumbled that it was taking too long. Finally she was tied to the stake. An English soldier took pity on her and handed her two small sticks lashed together to serve as a crucifix. Moments later the fire was lit. Most people who recorded their impressions of her last moments agree that she didn't scream in pain as the flames rose around her, but continued to pray.

Her executioner reported, "Once in the fire she cried out more than six times 'Jesus!' and especially in her last breath she cried out with a strong voice 'Jesus!' so that everyone present could hear it; almost all wept with pity."[3]

According to another account, "She was soon dead and her clothes were burned away; then they raked back the fire and showed her naked body to all the people. . . . When they had stared long enough at her dead corpse tied to the stake, the executioner got a big fire going again around her poor carcass and it was soon burned up, both flesh and bone reduced to ashes."[4]

The crowd—many of whose members had impatiently demanded her to be burned only a few minutes earlier—was impressed by the manner in which Joan had died. Even the doubters apparently had become convinced of her holiness. As a result, her executioners believed that it was important to eliminate all traces of her. Even a tiny fragment could serve as a relic and a rallying point. They gathered everything that remained and threw it into the Seine River. Within minutes, the last signs of Joan's earthly existence had vanished into its depths.

Did Joan Escape Her Execution?

There is no doubt that a woman was burned at the stake in Rouen on May 30, 1431. But was it Joan? A few people believe it wasn't.

They say that Joan wasn't born to Jacques and Isabelle d'Arc. Rather, they believe that her real parents were Isabeau of Bavaria—the wife of Charles VI—and Charles' brother Louis. Joan was born in 1407, not long after Louis was assassinated by his political enemies. The terrified Isabeau had to give up the child. One of her ladies-in-waiting was related to the d'Arc family. The baby was taken in secret to Domrémy. Jacques and Isabelle agreed to raise the little girl as if she were their own. It helped that they were given a large sum of money—both to cover the baby's expenses and to ensure their silence about the child's origins.

Charles VI

When Joan was captured, the main goal of the French was to make sure that she wasn't turned over to English church officials, who would have killed her. Therefore, Pierre Cauchon was actually acting out an elaborate charade during the months of the trial. He pretended to be a harsh prosecutor while he was actually making plans to save her. On the morning of her scheduled execution, Joan was secretly taken from her prison. A woman who had been convicted of witchcraft was substituted. She wore a hat and veil that concealed her features. By the time the unfortunate woman's execution was over, the flames had made her features completely unrecognizable.

Given her reprieve, Joan was married in 1436. She died thirteen years later of a fever. She had no children.

This theory was first published in 1805, and variations on the original idea have appeared ever since then. Most scholars dismiss it, with comments such as "For the theory to command credence, it must be accepted that Joan lied throughout her trial."[5] Perhaps the most important evidence against it is the record that a child was indeed born in 1407 to Isabeau and Louis. The infant's name was Philippe—a boy. By the time of the boy's birth, Louis was dead, so he had no more children.

This statue of Joan of Arc by Anna Hyatt, who was born in 1876, won an award in Paris in 1910. A replica of the statue currently stands in New York City. Hyatt created a number of other statues and sculptures before her death in 1973.

CHAPTER
FIVE

ST. JOAN

Joan's body may have been swallowed by fire and the Seine. Her spirit and her reputation were destined to live on.

As medieval military historian Kelly DeVries notes, "Joan's renown is attached to her military ability, to the skill she had in leading men into battle against great odds and possible death. This made the greatest influence on her time."[1]

Her prediction of a free France didn't take long to come true. The Duke of Burgundy gave his allegiance to Charles VII in 1436, which decisively changed the balance of power. Seventeen years later the English were driven from France, never to return as invaders. Shortly afterward they had their own civil war—the Wars of the Roses—which revolved around conflicting claims to the English throne. Henry VI—king of both England and France at his birth—would die at the hands of his enemies in the Tower of London in 1471 after losing both of those crowns.

Even before that happened, the effort to rehabilitate Joan's reputation had begun. Charles arrived in Rouen in triumph late in 1449. Two months later he ordered an inquiry into the original trial. He may have been motivated by less than idealistic reasons. He probably didn't want to have someone who was so closely connected with his rise to the throne to remain convicted of witchcraft and heresy. Several men who had been connected with the trial made statements to a panel of lawyers. The panel quickly issued an opinion that the trial had been unjust, but things went no further.

Two years later, Joan's mother, Isabelle, and her brothers appealed to have the case reopened. More than twenty witnesses appeared on Joan's behalf. Again the proceedings ground to a halt. Pope Nicholas V didn't want to risk offending the English.

Nicholas died in 1455. The new Pope, Calixtus III, was willing to reopen the case. It may have helped that many people who had participated in Joan's prosecution at the original trial—including Cauchon—were dead by that time. More than 150 witnesses—nearly all of them who had direct experience with Joan—gave testimony on her behalf and provided future generations with a great deal of information about her. No one testified against Joan. Her conviction in 1431 had been a foregone conclusion. Her acquittal appeared to be just as inevitable. On July 7, 1456, three representatives of the Pope joined with the Archbishop of Rheims and several other important church officials in a solemn ceremony. The Archbishop read aloud a statement that completely cleared Joan of any wrongdoing. A copy of the original accusation against her was ripped to shreds. Joan was rehabilitated.

More than 350 years later, a different Pope—Pius IX—became involved with Joan's case. In 1869, Bishop Dupanloup of Orléans and the bishops of eleven other cities that Joan had helped to liberate sent a petition to the Pope. They asked him to begin the process of declaring Joan as a saint of the Catholic Church. Unfortunately, the Franco-Prussian War—in which the German kingdom of Prussia quickly and easily defeated the French—began shortly afterward and deflected attention from the bishops' request. It was nearly forgotten. It wasn't until 1894 that Pope Leo XIII revived the proposal. From that point on, the proceedings moved rapidly ahead. The process was completed on May 16, 1920, when Pope Benedict XV canonized Joan of Arc. Now she was Saint Joan. Her feast day was declared as May 30, the day on which she had bravely faced the flames.

Joan's life is well-suited for dramatic presentations. In 1923, the famous playwright George Bernard Shaw wrote *Saint Joan*. Many people consider the play to be his finest work. Hollywood has also portrayed Joan on the silver screen on several occasions: *Joan the Woman* (1917), *Joan of Arc* (1948), and *Saint Joan* (1957).

Joan has been the subject of many paintings and other works of art. Two chapels in Rouen—one in the cathedral and the other on the site of her burning—are dedicated to her. A large statue of Joan holding a cross and mounted on a horse stands before the city hall in Vaucouleurs. She is especially revered in Orléans, where another statue of her on horseback is one of many reminders of her liberation of the city.

Not surprisingly, for a long time the English didn't share the same high regard for Joan as the French. The great English dramatist William Shakespeare portrayed Joan in a very unflattering manner in his play *Henry VI, Part 1*. He wasn't alone. For several centuries other English writers trashed her reputation. Eventually the English "forgave" her. When a huge celebration was held in Rouen on May 30, 1931, to honor the 500th anniversary of Joan's death, the Archbishop of Westminster was in attendance to represent the Church of England.

Meanwhile, the French government extended a great honor to Joan's memory. It declared May 8, the day on which she had been so instrumental in lifting the siege of Orléans, as a national holiday.

It is tragic that Joan died while she was still a teenager. In a few brief months of inspired leadership, she left behind a legacy that leads some historians to regard her as a role model for accomplishment by women. However, her bravery and her devotion to selfless ideals go beyond gender. She is an inspiration for anyone.

FYI
For Your Info

The Catholic Church places a great deal of importance on its saints. Catholics believe that saints not only serve as models of ideal human behavior, but also speak directly to God on behalf of seriously ill people.

Elizabeth Seton

For many years, people were declared as saints as a result of public acclaim. While this gave sainthood to many deserving people, sometimes legendary figures were declared as saints. Thus, in the tenth century, canonization—the process of recognizing saints—became the responsibility of church officials. Under their jurisdiction, canonization eventually became one of the world's most complicated and difficult legal procedures. The procedure has undergone several revisions, with the most recent occurring in 1983.

The first requirement is that a candidate for sainthood must have been dead for at least five years. The candidate must also have been a member of the Catholic Church. Once someone is nominated, a lengthy and exhaustive investigation into the person's life that often takes several years begins. If this investigation demonstrates that the person lived a life of extraordinary virtue, he or she is declared by the Pope to be "venerable."

The next step is to identify specific miraculous medical recoveries that can be attributed by praying to the venerable person. Physicians and religious authorities conclude that a miracle has occurred when there is no possible medical explanation for the person's being cured. According to Catholic belief, the cure demonstrates that the venerable person has spoken directly with God. The cure must be both instantaneous and complete. One candidate was rejected when a formerly blind person's sight was only 90 percent restored.

When one such miracle can be identified and verified, the person becomes beatified, or blessed. A second miracle leads to sainthood, or canonization. Catholics emphasize that the process of canonization does not create a saint. It reflects something that God has already done.

The majority of Catholic saints are European. Only one saint, Elizabeth Seton, was born in the United States.

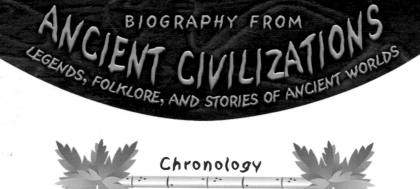
Chronology

1412		Joan is born on January 6 in Domrémy, France
1425		Hears voices for the first time
1428		Flees with family to Neufchâteau
1429	January	Leaves Domrémy for Vaucouleurs
	March	Meets Charles
	May	Helps raise siege of Orléans
	June	Helps win "week of victories"
	July	Attends crowning of Charles in Rheims
	September	Fails in attack on Paris
1430	May	Captured at Compiègne
	June	Taken to Beaurevoir
	December	Arrives in Rouen
1431	February	Trial for heresy begins
	May 30	Burned at the stake
1450		Inquiry into trial begins
1456		Acquitted of the charge of heresy
1869		Case for canonization comes before the Pope
1904		Declared venerable
1909		Is beatified
1920		Becomes saint in the Catholic Church

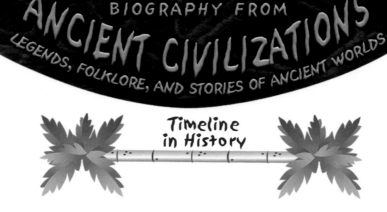

Timeline
in History

1314	The French King Philip IV dies.
1321	Italian poet Dante Alighieri publishes his *Divine Comedy.*
1337	The Hundred Years' War begins.
1347	The Black Plague, which kills millions of people in Europe, begins.
1375	Robin Hood appears in English popular literature.
1387	English poet Geoffrey Chaucer begins writing *the Canterbury Tales.*
1403	French King Charles VII is born.
1415	English King Henry V defeats the French at the Battle of Agincourt.
1420	Henry V marries Catherine of France and enters Paris.
1422	Henry V dies and is succeeded by his nine-month-old son, Henry VI.
1453	The Hundred Years' War ends, as England gives up all its French territory except the port of Calais.
1455	The Wars of the Roses begin in England as two rival factions claim the throne.
1461	Charles VII dies.
1471	English King Henry VI is murdered in the Tower of London.
1480	Italian inventor and artist Leonardo da Vinci invents an early form of the parachute.
1492	Christopher Columbus discovers the New World.
1503	Leonardo da Vinci paints *Mona Lisa,* one of the world's most famous works of art.
1508	Italian painter, sculptor, and architect Michelangelo Buonarroti begins painting the Sistine Chapel.
1527	Rome is attacked by soldiers of the Holy Roman Empire, ending the Italian Renaissance.

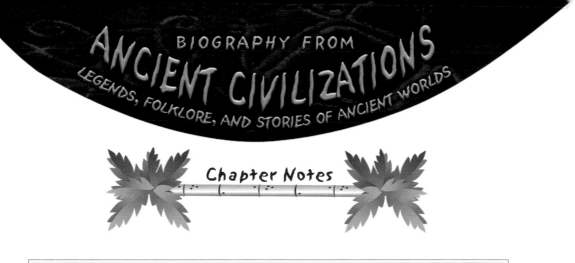

Chapter Notes

CHAPTER 1
A TANGLED WEB
1. Mary Gordon, *Joan of Arc* (New York: Viking, 2000), p. 56.
2. The Avalon Project at Yale Law School: "The Salic Law," http://www.yale.edu/lawweb/avalon/medieval/salic.htm

CHAPTER 2
HEEDING THE VOICE OF GOD
1. Joan of Arc, *Joan of Arc in Her Own Words,* translated by Willard Trask (New York: Turtle Point, 1996), p. 3.
2. Regine Pernoud, *Joan of Arc: By Herself and Her Witnesses,* translated by Edward Hyams (New York: Stein and Day, 1966), p. 18.
3. Ibid.
4. Joan of Arc, *Joan of Arc in Her Own Words,* translated by Willard Trask (New York: Turtle Point, 1996), pp. 5–6.
5. Ibid., p. 7.
6. Ibid., p. 11.
7. Andrea Hopkins, *Most Wise and Valiant Ladies* (New York: Welcome Rain, 1997), p. 15.
8. W. S. Scott, *Jeanne d'Arc* (London: George G. Harrap & Co. Ltd., 1974), pp. 35–36.

9. Ibid., p. 40.
10. Ibid., p. 43.

CHAPTER 3
FROM VICTOR TO VICTIM
1. Andrea Hopkins, *Most Wise and Valiant Ladies* (New York: Welcome Rain, 1997), p. 20.
2. Mary Gordon, *Joan of Arc* (New York: Viking, 2000), p. 56.

CHAPTER 4
A HORRIBLE DEATH, BY FIRE
1. Andrea Hopkins, *Most Wise and Valiant Ladies* (New York: Welcome Rain, 1997), p. 31.
2. Regine Pernoud, *Joan of Arc: By Herself and Her Witnesses,* translated by Edward Hyams (New York: Stein and Day, 1966), p. 221.
3. Mary Gordon, *Joan of Arc* (New York: Viking, 2000), p. 129.
4. Andrea Hopkins, *Most Wise and Valiant Ladies* (New York: Welcome Rain, 1997), p. 11.
5. Marina Warner, *Joan of Arc: The Image of Female Heroism* (New York: Alfred A. Knopf, 1981), p. 59.

CHAPTER 5
ST. JOAN
1. Kelly DeVries, *Joan of Arc: A Military Leader* (Phoenix Mill, United Kingdom: Sutton Publishing Limited, 1999), p. 187.

For Further Reading

For Young Adults

Brooks, Polly Schoyer. *Beyond the Myth: The Story of Joan of Arc.* New York: Houghton Mifflin, 1999.

Lace, William. *Joan of Arc and the Hundred Years' War in World History.* Berkeley Heights, New Jersey: Enslow Publishers, 2003.

Murpurgo, Michael. *Joan of Arc.* New York: Harcourt Brace and Company, 1999.

Nardo, Don. *The Trial of Joan of Arc.* San Diego, California: Lucent Books, 1997.

Pickels, Dwayne. *Joan of Arc.* Broomall, Pennsylvania: Chelsea House, 2001.

Roberts, Jeremy. *Saint Joan of Arc.* Minneapolis, Minnesota: Lerner Publications, 2000.

Stanley, Diane. *Joan of Arc.* New York: HarperCollins, 1995.

Wallace, Susan Helen. *Saint Joan of Arc, God's Soldier.* Boston: Pauline Books and Media, 2000.

Works Consulted

David-Darnac, Maurice. *The True Story of the Maid of Orleans.* Translated by Peter de Polnay. London: W. H. Allen, 1969.

DeVries, Kelly. *Joan of Arc: A Military Leader.* Phoenix Mill, United Kingdom: Sutton Publishing Limited, 1999.

Gordon, Mary. *Joan of Arc.* New York: Viking, 2000.

Hopkins, Andrea. *Most Wise and Valiant Ladies.* New York: Welcome Rain, 1997.

Joan of Arc. *Joan of Arc in Her Own Words.* Translated by Willard Trask. New York: Turtle Point, 1996.

Pernoud, Regine. *Joan of Arc: By Herself and Her Witnesses.* Translated by Edward Hyams. New York: Stein and Day, 1966.

Scott, W. S. *Jeanne d'Arc.* London: George G. Harrap & Co. Ltd., 1974.

Warner, Marina. *Joan of Arc: The Image of Female Heroism.* New York: Alfred A. Knopf, 1981.

On the Internet

"All About . . . The Loire"
http://www.visaloire.com/ loire.php?lang=en

The Avalon Project at Yale Law School: "The Salic Law"
http://www.yale.edu/lawweb/avalon/ medieval/salic.htm

Catholic Encyclopedia: "St. Catherine of Alexandria"
http://www.newadvent.org/cathen/ 03445a.htm

Catholic Encyclopedia: "St. Joan of Arc"
http://www.newadvent.org/cathen/ 08409c.htm

Catholic Encyclopedia: "St. Margaret"
http://www.newadvent.org/cathen/ 09652b.htm

For Further Reading

Eternal Word Television Network: "St. Michael—Archangel"
http://www.ewtn.com/library/MARY/MICHAEL.htm

International Joan of Arc Society
http://www.smu.edu/ijas

Joan of Arc Online Archive
http://archive.joan-of-arc.org

"Joan's Journey to Canonization"
http://www.stjoan-center.com/novelapp/joaap04.html

Miracles: "Sainthood 101: Rules for Becoming a Saint"
http://www.sonyclassics.com/thethirdmiracle/mir-sainthood101.html

Picch, Ryan. "Becoming a Saint."
http://www.procopius.org/CampusCatholic/cc2-2/2-2vii.htm

Portraits of a Saint: "Becoming a Saint"
http://saint-joan-of-arc.com/becoming-a-saint.htm

Glossary

acclaimed (uh-KLAMED)—highly praised.
anointed (uh-NOIN-ted)—rubbed with oil during a solemn ritual.
archangel (ark-ANE-gel)—a chief angel.
besieged (bee-SEEJ'D)—to be surrounded by armed forces.
courtiers (KOR-tee-uhrs)—persons, usually noblemen and noblewomen, in attendance at a royal court.
credence (CREE-dunts)—believability.
dauphin (doe-FAN)—the eldest son of a French king.
dynasty (DIE-nuh-stee)—a succession of rulers from a common ancestor.
pagan (PAY-gun)—a person who believes in several gods or in no religion at all.
pious (PIE-us)—showing a high degree of reverence for a deity.
reprieve (ree-PREEVE)—a delay of punishment for a crime; a break.
vow of chastity (CHAS-tuh-tee)—a promise never to have sexual relationships.

Index